WILD CINNAMON AND WINTER SKIN

ALSO BY SENI SENEVIRATNE

Climbing Mountains, poetry and song collection, audio tape (collaboration with Maya Chowdhry).

Her poems have been featured in:
Masala: Poems from India, Bangladesh, Pakistan & Sri Lanka (Macmillan Children's Books); *Healing Strategies for Women at War* (Cultureword); *Talking Black* (Cassell); *Kiss* (Cultureword); *Flora Poetica* (Chatto & Windus); *As Girls Could Boast* (Oscars Press); *Bad Reputation* (Yorkshire Arts Circus); *Nailing Colours* (Crocus Books); *Flora Poetica* (Chatto & Windus); *The Redbeck Anthology of British South Asian Poetry* (Redbeck Press); *Miscegenation Blues* (Sister Vision Press); *A woman sits down to write* (WWWCape Town); *Daskhat Journal* (Denmark).

SENI SENEVIRATNE

WILD CINNAMON AND WINTER SKIN

PEEPAL TREE

First published in Great Britain in 2007
Peepal Tree Press Ltd
17 King's Avenue
Leeds LS6 1QS
UK

ISBN 1 84523 050 7
ISBN 13: 978 184523 05 0

Peepal Tree gratefully acknowledges Arts Council support

ACKNOWLEDGEMENTS

Thank you to the following for their belief, time and support in me and in the making of this collection: Kadija Sesay and Inscribe, Nathalie Handal, Mimi Khalvati, Jacob Ross, Jeremy Poynting and Hannah Bannister at Peepal Tree Press, Pete Kalu at Cultureword.

Thank you to the following for inspiration, encouragement and shared celebration of my writing self:

my mother and father, Winnie and Chris; my daughter, Kate; my granddaughter, Annie; family and friends in UK, Turkey, Sri Lanka, South Africa and Australia.

Special thanks to Tanya Chan-Sam, Maya Chowdhry and Chloe Balcomb who have been invaluable and inspirational writing companions on this long journey.

With loving memory for my parents, for Kate Truscott and for Marie Miles.

Some of these poems have featured in the following publications and broadcasts: *Nailing Colours*, *Flora Poetica*, *The Redbeck Anthology of British South Asian Poetry*, *Healing Strategies for Women at War*, *Miscegenation Blues*, *A woman sits down to write*, BBC Radio 4 Talking Poetry. *Cinnamon Roots* won second prize in the Margot Jane Memorial Poetry Prize, Onlywomen Press. *Dandelion Clocks,* performed at the Leeds Leider Festival 2005 with piano and voice and *A Wider View*, performed at Leeds Music College in 2006 accompanied by a saxophone quartet, are collaborative pieces with musician and composer Gemma Wild.

For Tanya,
for all the years we've shared,
for all the words we've weaved,
for always.

CONTENTS

OPUS TESSELATUM

Diminutive tesserae, bright shards of marble
and glass paste – copper, cobalt, nickel, gold
and lapis lazuli. My fingers, sticky with Pliny's
mortar, three parts sand to one part lime,
bind the fragments of my shattered history.

Terracotta cones play geometric games
with pebbled stone and random shells
in landscapes of enamel, where a flax dresser
combs the bark of linum trees, lays it out
on grass to bleach its yellow fibres linen white,
breaks and swingles with the swipple of his flail.
Ready for the loom, it makes a canvas for
the seamstress, embroidering familiar gardens
with her alphabet of stitches; who takes the pen
from the fingers of the registrar and holds it,
like a needle, above inky swirls of red and black.
Her eyes close to the paper, she copies
a cross-stitch to mark her name.

Tessellated tales of agate, boiled in sugar,
stained as black as onyx, pave the path
of a sea-captain, landlocked by grief,
who trails three motherless daughters
across the Pennines, to Yorkshire,
where a boot finisher, eighteen years old,
abandons his waxing wheel to join
a Regiment of Foot, and wear out
thirteen pairs of regulation army soles
to defend the British Raj.

Pictographs in amethyst and turquoise,
set at angles, catch the light in the courts
of Seethawaka. A Mudliyar strokes

the gold of his brocaded sash and dreams
of grazing water buffalo in the hills of Rakwana,
where a mother, haunted by a vision of an upturned
rickshaw, bows her head before the wisdom
of the astrologer's charts, to save her unborn son.

Ochre-tinted grout smooths the rough edge of
voices in the family of a lawyer's daughter.
She discards her Burgher name for love of
a Sinhala, a poet buried under
too many letters of the law, a barrister
paid by the poor with sacks of mangosteens.

The stories coil like ammonite, are etched in epitaphs
sealed in unmarked graves, stamped on soldiers' passbooks
released from faded photographs, whispered through the centuries.
I gather every bright shard, collect every broken piece,
wash and polish, press them into place.
The mortar is damp and yields to the touch.

A WIDER VIEW

From the backyard of his back-to-back,
my great-great-granddad searched for spaces
in the smoke-filled sky to stack his dreams,
high enough above the cholera to keep them
and his newborn safe from harm.

In eighteen sixty-nine, eyes dry with dust
from twelve hours combing flax beneath
the conicals of light in Marshall's Temple Mill,
he took the long way home because
he craved the comfort of a wider view.

As he passed the panelled gates of Tower Works,
the tall octagonal crown of Harding's chimney
drew his sights beyond the limits of his working life
drowned the din of engines, looms and shuttles
with imagined peals of ringing bells.

Today, my footsteps echo in the sodium gloom
of Neville Street's Dark Arches and the red-brick vaults
begin to moan as time, collapsing in the River Aire,
sweeps me out to meet him on the Wharf.

We stand now, timeless in the flux of time, anchored
only by the axis of our gaze – a ventilation shaft
with gilded tiles, and Giotto's geometric lines –
while the curve of past and future generations
arcs between us.

LENA RULAK

Who are you Lena Rulak?
Mother of my father, daughter of a lawyer,
Eurasian Burgher of Sri Lanka.

You are my father's speechless memories
moving through me, like the sea,
in my restless sleep.

You wrap me in his body, clothe me in words
that have wandered through oceans,
wash me up on the dream tide.

Your arms are wide and change the blue
to gold. You treasure me in smells of spices and kindness,
cradle me in a language I never knew,
turn my questions into songs.

Looking through the mist,
I see him, twelve years old,
wipe confusion from his eyes.
They are deep brown questions
piercing the freezing haze of
a colourless winter, wondering
where the green disappears
in the strange cobbled streets,
asking why his father went
and why his mother died.

He sailed on the *Orama*
across the Indian ocean.
Savoured the last taste
of the mango sunsets of Sri Lanka,
lost his tears in sharp sea spray,
found his mother in a dream of home.
Locked her in his heart
with the keys of a religion
that had travelled East from Portugal,
four hundred years before.

He sailed beyond Portugal,
saw his mother rise from the waters
of the Indian and Atlantic Oceans,
and promise to stay with him.
He brought his white gods
home to England's winter
where skies, like dirty blankets,
covered people with frozen smiles,
who had no rice flour or rickshaws
and burnt black rocks to keep them warm.

He saw his father marry
a white child-bride, sail back to the East,
leaving him to dream of
ocean liners and Colombo streets,
leaving him, in exchange,
with a white-girl's parents,
leaving him to become the odd-boy-out,
the black face in the school photo,
the curiosity, holding onto his religion
as a passport to acceptance.

Looking through the mist,
I find his puzzled face
reflecting mine, scouring the years
for my own hazy history –
sepia photos, silken saris
and half-told stories.
But I can't see far enough,
never asked the questions
to know how he lived,
through so many losses and leavings.

BLOOD RED DROWNING

They cut my mother. Saved our lives
in a sudden blast of light and cold air.

Hungry for warmth, I craved skin.
Was cradled under a glass quilt.

A pink blanket — for her baby's shroud?
Blood-stained prayers — too late to save?

Her fears sewn behind the scars,
she never found a way to tell.

Mine were mute. I carried them all
wrapped in tight bundles around my back,

crying for comfort, rocked to fitful sleep.
Wanted, nearly lost, rejected, over-protected.

Hero and villain of family stories,
I never found a way to make amends

to her, who never made amends to me
who both only needed to accept the pain,

blood red, in which we drowned.

BROWN PAPER CAMEO

For my mother

She who covers her
sighs with noise, follows the dust
into corners, moves

with wings through a house,
sprinkling songs on carpet pile
to cover the sound

of daily living,
can't find her way back to the
taste of her own heartbeat.

YORKSHIRE CHILDHOOD

Swings and roundabouts across the road,
at the end of a cobbled street, down steep
steps from a scullery, with a sink too high
and a bucket underneath. Out of a back room
with a shiny black fireplace filled with red hot –
Don't touch! Don't stand too near!
as I held the toasting fork to brown the pikelets.

My brown hands were stinging with the heat,
red face beaming as I waited for melting
butter over licking lips. I disappeared then
into a worn armchair, but never my Grandad's.
That waited empty, like his slippers, till he arrived
to eat his dinner, always ready on the table, and drink
his gravy from the plate – though we were never allowed.

My grandma taught me to make egg custard
tarts, very carefully. Said I had pastry fingers.
My brown hands dipped in and out of fatty flour
moulding, rolling – like her fingers that she
worked to the bone, so she wore a gap in the
gold of her ring (when I always thought
gold was too hard to wear out).

My grandma wore pink corsets, laughed at
her own long baggy knickers, let me snuggle up
to her bum in bed, told me I was important
and special; that no matter what anyone said
or teased, I had a right to be who I was, and
that I would be great, I would be wonderful,
I would show them all in the end just how good I was,
my brown hands reaching across the mound of her belly.

FRAME YOURSELF

When my mother said *Frame yourself,* my sister and I
would stare at each other, trying to keep our faces straight,
and draw a frame in mid-air. We pinned our mouths
shut to suppress the laughter as she hurried us into
sensible school shoes that were wide enough for our feet
because she knew what it was like to nurse corns and blisters.
The radio was always playing some sweet music and the numbers
on the front never made sense as the needle whizzed past them.
First a crackle, then a strong signal that brought clear sound
so we turned our ears towards it, and were still not ready.

THE ORPHAN DOLL

My mother always told me *Hold your sister's hand*
and hurry home from school, don't linger.
But on that day in nineteen fifty-six, the broken house
next to the four-a-penny sweet shop made us stop.
It smelled of *Don't go in there,* held us helpless in its
rotted doorway, sherbet lemon fizzing on our tongues.

I saw her then, the orphan doll, abandoned in the dust
between the damaged floorboards. Her blue eyes stared
right into my soul, set off a flock of birds inside my head
(so I couldn't hear my mother's *Hurry home from school*),
made me linger, wriggled my fingers free, pulled me
from my sister's grasp towards her waiting eyes.

I almost reached her, almost saved her from the dust
and smell. But my sister, fuelled by her duties,
cautioned by the certainty of blame,
caught the hem of my coat and dragged me back so hard
I fell and all the four-a-penny sweets went rolling
from my pockets down the street, like guilty secrets.

ONT' SAFE SIDE

It's not usual for me to drink me glass o' Guinness
int' afternoon but today's different. They'll all laugh
at me when they get 'ere, sitting int' freezin' cold,
both doors wide open and rainin' buckets outside.

Our Cissy wouldn't laugh, Lord rest her soul.

There it goes again. It's so loud now, like it's
pickin' up me 'ouse and shakin' it. They'll think
I'm daft, but I'm glad I shut curtains.
I'll have another sip o' Guinness.

I need through-draught y' see to be ont' safe side.
That way, when thunderbolt comes down chimney,
it's sucked straight out, through one o' doors.
They won't understand.

Our Cissy would though, Lord rest her soul.

She'd remember tale our mam told us about thunderbolt
roarin' down our cobbled backstreet, smashin' railin's
on East End Park. Council never did put 'em back.
Now where's me drink?

They'll all be back soon, fillin' me 'ouse
wi' grandkids and Sunday tea.
I'll just sit tight, say some prayers and
hide me Guinness behind Our Lady's picture.

Our Cissy'll watch over me, Lord rest her soul.

GRANDAD'S INSULIN

Nineteen fifty-five. I am four years old.
The tablecloth is flecked with crumbs and
smudged with tea-time sauce. The cupboard's closed
on piles of jumbled toys and the silent wireless
stares down on me with pale eyes.

Knees and bottom cling to the comfy feel
of well-worn carpet's swirls – gold on red.
My legs fanned out on either side, I trace
one finger, seeking out smooth islands
where the pile has left this tufted ocean.

The old man breathing in a high green chair
has hands like my dad, but his eyes are browner
and his hair is greyer. He came last night with
stories, presents, kisses to cover my shyness.
I don't know him. My Grandad from Ceylon.

He has a box today. Black. Leather. And when
he leans, those hands like my father's
click the silver lock, flip the lid. The treasure
of red lining pulls my finger off its course
towards the feel of velvet.

I rub, in steady, solid, up-and-down, side-to-side
strokes. The way it smooths and roughs itself
on my skin. I try not to look at the needle on a tube,
like in my brother's doctor set, but bigger.
Try to keep my eyes on the carpet,

so I won't follow his hands, like my fathers,
as they raise the needle high above me.
Try to pull my eyes back to the velvet

to the red, where my finger's motion
is steadying me, so I won't see

the brown of his skin, as he dabs with cotton wool,
or the plunge of the needle, that makes my finger
stop short. And a voice like mine from far away
shouts *Oh* as my eyes squeeze themselves tight,
trying to see his ship coming over the sea

from a place I've only seen in picture books,
or the white blonde walking-doll he brought me,
but all I see is the needle piercing his skin.

REMEMBERED RASPBERRIES

As children we gathered raspberries, foraging through
the jungle of bushes halfway down our garden.
Six eyes searched the tangled green for flash of red.
Never mind the prickles, the stinging weals along our arms and legs
were worth the prize we carried whole into our mouths,
where impatient tongues pressed each precious bubble
into tiny tremors of delight, until we overflowed with juices.

But still, we had bowlfuls left to carry proudly
to my father's kitchen (his domain only on jam-making day)
where the pressure cooker steamed and gurgled high above us.
We swayed on tiptoe, stretched our eyes to watch the treasures
tumble into bubbling sticky heat, until his words, *Stand back,*
before those bubbles burn and peel your skin away in layers,
chased us, shrieking, from the danger to the dining table.

There, our restless, red-stained fingers daubed the sterile jars,
toyed with kits of rubber seals, elastic bands and greaseproof
paper circles. We squirmed and learned to wait for jam
to cook and cool. Later, spoon by spoon, we filled the jars
to just below the rim, sealed the summer, stored it airtight
on the highest shelf, in the cupboard under the stairs.

PIPE CLEANER PERMS

Delivered from the trauma of a drowning birth
by the cold steel of surgical knives, maybe
my soft black curls were shock waves,
baby curls peeping from fluffy bonnets,
toddler curls pointing wildly in all directions.
By three they were pulled tight from a straight
side parting into a bow as big as my head,
stray hairs clamped with clips and slides.
The curls sighed, gave up, withered to a subtle kink.

At five, home perm kits coaxed them back. Toni,
Rayve, Bobbi, Twink, my mother tried them all.
Memories of first communions, Whitsuntides,
Christmas family gatherings tinged with smells
more putrid than a stink bomb. I gagged in fumes
beneath my mother's fingers as she sponged
small strands of hair with alkaline, folded tissue
end-papers and rolled them up in pipe cleaners
flat against my head in rows right up to my parting.

My body fidgeted, shifted on the seat, my hands
scratched the tickles in my bottom, my legs
danced over the edge of the dining room chair.
My head, in the firm grip of my mother's hands,
stayed still. Eyes closed tight against the sting,
nose wrinkled against the stench, scalp fried
under the relentless heat of the Morphy Richards dryer,
I savoured the anticipation of the froth of frizzy curls
that would billow from my side parting.

EIGHTEEN
For Kate

Roses shout above a table filled with this year's
birthday breakfast – ripe strawberries, flushed cherries,
blushing plums – to mark your eighteen years of growing
under my watchful eyes.

Now you dance out of my reach, a woman from my blood,
popping with passion, aglow in the heat of future plans.
You drape the crimson shawl of my love around you,
gaze beyond my horizons, leave my nest.

I remember the velvet of your luscious baby skin,
born on a silent morning, coaxed to cry, blue feet
turning pink. Today red celebrates your arrival
at the door to tomorrow.

DANDELION CLOCKS

For Annie Kaya

In my garden, she crawls small
amongst tall grass, dandelion clocks
like fluffy moons above her head.
She blows and silky plumes
stick to her lips, hover in her chuckle,
dappled wishes, heartbeats of delight,
before the clutter of words.

Her fingertips, as small as bluebell cups,
trace round and round the garden of my
cradling palm, unravelling my lifeline.
And drifting dandelion seeds
count time backwards, replanting me
in the red earth of my own beginning.

SOMETHING IN THE AIR

There's something in the air
between us, you said,
makes it difficult to talk,
about anything.

At least that's something,
I thought, I was beginning
to feel like there's nothing
between us any more.

And the moon on the water
was moving with the ripples
and everything we said
kept moving on, in circles.

LOVER'S NEVER MEAN TO LIE

Mouths are full of cells more complex than
the simple chlamydomonas
— a word that helps even the cockroach
of the algae world sound chic.

Mouths can make luscious purple promises
then pop your expectations like a balloon
with a single word shorter than the bleep
of an electrocardiogram.

The word mouth may not be palindromic
but it can look the same from both sides
and take words with metronomic regularity
around the rotunda of conversations.

Lovers never mean to lie;
it's just the way the words come alive
like wriggling metatarsals in their mouths.

DARNED SOCKS AND CHRISTMAS LIGHTS

Litany for a doomed love affair

You're the maple leaves scorched by sun
You're jam and butter without the toast
You're the signpost going nowhere
You're the crumbled cliffs on the wet East coast

You're a puncture kit without the glue
You're the brambles in a fuschia hedge
You're the splinters in a hand-carved bench
You're the mountain climb without a ledge

You're the darned sock that came undone
You're the pavement stone that didn't fit
You're the picnic spot without a view
You're the Christmas lights I never lit

You're the torn seat in a railway carriage
You're the Ming vase that slipped and fell
You're the twisted ankle on a country walk
You're the worn-out games of kiss and tell

PURPLE HEART

I am lazy as the Zambesi,
I drift, tread water, wait
for the rushing, roaring, falling
that may be just round the corner.

My heart has grown purple with longing,
but July comes and goes each year
and still no lover paints her pleasure
on my skin.

Some nights she comes and seasons my dreams,
finds me dallying in Colombo streets,
leaves the print of her hand in my palm,
the curve of her skin on my back,
the breath of her kiss on my neck,
but her face always escapes me.

NEXT TIME

I was a desert, shut tight against
the winds of nostalgia,
until you came, in an African winter,
beating at my heart's drum
to let you in from the cold.
I thought your body would turn to dust,
like the lover in my dreams,
but your skin was warm,
flowing through my hands,
covering every inch of me,
watering my dry, making all my
passion flowers bloom.

LONG DISTANCE

We met like two oceans at Cape Point
and our waves were breaking over
cautious questions as we drifted into
easy days, fingering the smell
of growing passion, running wild
against the storms on Noordhoek beach
that stretched far beyond our shadows.

When I left, the sky was blood orange.

Now I eat your words for breakfast,
after nightime travels, where I find you
sleeping under the mountain fynbos.
I dazzle your eyes with shining seaweed
and drench your dreams in jasmine
memories, too strong to fade.

SEARCHING IN AN ENGLISH GARDEN
FOR A LOVE POEM

Dandelions punctuate the grass. Lost for words,
I stare from the gazebo at the promise of magnolia,
an archway still to flower, empty summer house
beyond an aging wall, a veil of moss on stones.
April in Devon and I know I do not love you like
these faint whispers of an English early spring.

I love you like that first July in Jo'burg,
with all the clamour of the street traders and
the winter sky as blue as the roses on your curtains.

I love you like the seasons turned upside down,
like the long wait between letters,
like holding my breath until we touched again.

Now in the grey days of your exile
I love you so close that our borders blur
and the details threaten to fly from my desperate pages.

So I pin it down, this love, like pressed flowers.
Prized protea, crimson and sturdy, seeded by fire,
strutting strelitzia, bird of paradise petals flying,
long-stemmed agapanthus, hiding its resilience –
and the showy blooms of Namaqualand daisies
giving every bend in our road a surprise of colour.

BENEATH THE WATERFALL
Lumb Bank 1990

A tall black woman came to me the first night,
and I knew the house was full of spirits.

These days have stretched my tired mind
like a roll of white paper. The words fall
over me like droplets. I'm crouching
beneath the waterfall.

Wrapped in an Indian shawl, I have toasted
crumpets on an open fire, caressed your taste
buds with coconut dahl, strained to link
my mixed-up past with yours,

ghosts and vampires of my childhood nightmares
becoming the loupgarou and soucouyant to weave
our stories round.

One night, I caught a glimpse of my Sri Lankan
father in the face of a Caribbean poet,
saw Asia melt into Africa.

Each night I bathe in rosemary oil,
next day trawl my mind for images.

Loupgarou – werewolf
Soucouyant – vampire

EARLY MORNING HAIKUS

On the woodland walk
Crumpled orange crisp packet
Mocks nature's order

Picking cow parsley
Whispers of superstition
Prickle my fingers

On the stony path
A broken bird is a feast
For bluebottle flies

Inside my body
A gathering sneeze waits
To break the silence

Outside my body
The light grows in tangled trees
Branches like wishbones

Sunlight turns dull stone
to laser lights criss-crossing
under bronze water

SPEM IN ALIUM – MOTET FOR 40 VOICES
(Millennium Gallery – Sheffield)

The boy's ear is close to a speaker, he laughs,
skips away, then back, away, then back, away
like a firefly, his red jacket illuminating the room.

His girlfriend's rose-coloured dreads are gathered
in bunches and she runs at him, jumps, hugs him
in the centre of this circle of speakers.

The music stops. I wait. I listen to the cough
and shuffle of voices waiting to begin again.
The excited couple run from speaker to speaker.

I watch the effect of sound on them as I feel its
effect on me. They are moving sculptures in this
installation of sound, treading diverse harmonies,

while the curator sleeps in the corner.

THE WORLD OVER
For my Auntie G.

It's strange the way my life's bent double;
past and present face to face in the TV lounge
where departed friends and family collide with
smiling carers bringing half-filled cups of tepid tea.
It's strange, but why should I lock them out?

Lock them out? We never kept anyone out.
My grandma's scullery house had rubber walls;
door were always open. Not like these windows
always shut because that one, with too much to say
for herself, complains about the draught.

Door were always open. We never left that house
and we didn't know poverty. My dad was out of work
but I always took *my* tuppence to school. She had the
purse. Lived and died in that house with all of us round her.
I don't want to die here, in a house full of strangers.

Lived and died in that house. Strange, the way life
takes different turns. I can't grumble, got my own room
but no lock. No privacy and you can't trust strangers,
not like family. Besides, some of them are not all there.
I wave and they smile but that's about it.

Not all there. Lost touch with reality. That's what
them carers think of me. But I know what's what.
I might be a bit deaf, but I'm not daft. Sometimes
I dream and wake up confused. Doesn't everyone do that?
Wake up and take a while to get your bearings?

I wake up confused; think I'm late for work; wonder if
I've polished dad's boots by the fireside, where he left
them every night. Just me and him after Mam died.
This lot chuck my memories in the bin like used tea bags.
That's no way to carry on. I've lost nine people.

In the bin like used tea bags. It's my sister I miss most;
we made a good team – her legs, my brains. Life's strange.
Seventeen I was, just got off the tram on Lupton Avenue
when the motorbike hit me. A silver plate in my leg to rivet
my bones. I lost my youth on them tramlines.

Lost my youth on them tramlines. *She* married an Indian.
We just accepted it. You never thought ought about it.
It were just a situation. I helped her write the letters when
he went away to war. She'd ask me *What have I to put in
here now?* You just got on with living in them days.

Just got on with living. There's a scar. It covers up alright
with good quality nylons. Me mam said, *Hold your head up
and never let yourself go.* I'm just another old lady to them,
in the TV lounge waiting for me pills. I used to go everywhere.
I can't complain. I still have me hair done once a week.

I used to go everywhere. They think I've had a boring life.
but we made our own fun in them days. I used to go hiking.
That were before me accident. I've outlived all them hikers.
I loved Ireland. I once stood on the cliffs at Ballycastle
and heard silence for the first time; the silence of air.

I loved Ireland. Must be my granddad's Irish blood in me.
He died young, collapsed he did, in a church parade.
Served in India before that. India you see. It all interlocks.
We can't get away from it. It's a small world going round
in circles and people are the same the world over.

It's a small world. I stay in bed late now. They come
with tea in the morning. That's nice, being waited on.
I can't fault the place. You can come and go as you please.
Three meals a day, though my appetite's not what it was.
Some people use it more like a hotel. I can't grumble.

I can't grumble. We were never short of love. Me mam
could love a lot. Me dad could love but didn't show it.
He'd say, *I feel like cutting me throat,* and me mam
would hand him a carving knife, tell him to get on with it.
He had these moods; he were ruled by the moon, they said.

Feel like cutting me throat. *I know those moods alright*
I've been inside one. It's something on you. You don't talk,
you suffer. You can't get out from under it. You destroy
yourself and everyone round you knows it, sees it.
Only once I was in one. Never again, never again.

You don't talk, you suffer. Our doctor once said I were
backbone of my family. Life's strange. I'm getting tired
keeping upright but I can't complain. I'm getting on nicely
enough. People ruled by the moon, eh. In this day and age
they'd call it depression. I don't know, it's the world over.

BUNGEE JUMP

A rush of adrenalin through every cell,
a blur of grey, green, blue through open eyes,
a stomach lurch that squeezes them shut.
Red swirls behind closed lids, wisps of black hair
stream above her. She watches herself fall until
the pull of the harness hauls her inside her body.
Her mouth stretches in a scream, the sound left
somewhere in the air above her.

Her body is a swirling torrent, her heart stopped
mid-beat inside a held breath. Adrenalin churns
and multiplies, suspended on the whim of a cable.
Free-falling, she tracks a safe passage through
identical patterns of sensation, harnessed in this
purchased thrill anticipating the pleasure of the
final suspended moment.

Time shifts, nudged by body memories; the pressure
of a clammy hand across her jaw; the edge of a
forefinger pushing up against her nostrils; the sour
taste of sweat clawing the roof of her mouth.
A freeze frame of fear. Her life out of control.
Survival instinct shut down, waiting for the inevitable.
No pull on a cable to save her, free-falling to death.

The harness strains against her ribs, jerks her back
to real time, where her feet dangle high above the
shredded memories; eyes that flashed with desperation;
sinews tearing in her shoulder as he wrenched her bag;
gravel embedded in her elbow as she crashed to the ground.
Fragments of memory drift down the mountain slopes,
pieces of a torn photograph disappearing from her line of vision.
They come to rest. Find familiar hiding places to lie in wait.

She hangs. Her body's physical responses disconnect
from emotion and memory. Her heart kicks back
into a pounding rhythm. Her breath bellows in and out
of heaving lungs. A charge of survival froths into a
crescendo that overwhelms all her anxieties.

She plans her next jump. Along the coast, somewhere.
Off a bridge, 216 metres. The world's highest
bungee jump.

BEHIND CLOSED DOORS

Doors suffer
when no-one opens them.
Hinges rust, keys stay in locks,
nothing moves through them.

Reluctant jailers
of imprisoned secrets,
they groan against
the weight of untold stories.

Their wood yearns
for the touch of a passing hand,
the whisper of air. They want to fly open,
release sounds, bring air to musty rooms.

If keys were turned
and handles grasped, their suffering
would end. There'd be no secrets
behind closed doors.

MY FATHER'S UNCUT GEMS

Rubies,
stones of loss, filled with fire-words taunt my
growing up with everything my father never
told me, throw me from one colour of missing
to another, dare me to catch the fire. Burn my palms.

Pearls'
elusive emotions float in sea tears undiscovered.
Like an oyster-catcher, I dive, but the weight of
the ocean rejects me. I travel to wilder shores,
wait like a scavenger for washed-up shells.

Diamonds
say love like a cliché. My fingers search through
tangles of stories where lover's memories make
sharp reflections, like birds trailing their own
image. An illusion of two in still water.

PANTOUM
December 26th 2004

My father's birthplace has been swamped by a tsunami
The mouth of Kalu Ganga rendered mute
As the sea gods woke and raised an army
To settle an old boundary dispute

The mouth of Kalu Ganga rendered mute
Choked by bodies tumbling in the sea's attack
To settle an old boundary dispute
Kalutara shoreline driven back

Choked by bodies tumbling in the sea's attack
The cemetery submerged, Galle Road station crumbled
Kalutara shoreline driven back
At the river's source Sri Pada stumbled

The cemetery submerged, Galle Road station crumbled
Tourists credit cards were spat out on the beach
At the river's source Sri Pada stumbled
A place of safety was beyond the pilgrims' reach

Tourists credit cards were spat out on the beach
As the sea gods woke and raised an army
A place of safety was beyond the pilgrims' reach
My father's birthplace has been swamped by a tsunami.

Kalu Ganga – Black River
Sri Pada – Sacred footprint

44

WHAT DID YOU DO IN THE WAR, DAD?

I fought in the desert, one of Monty's boys,
green khaki camouflaging the
dusty brown of my skin.

They called me *The Chocolate Soldier,*
I laughed. They didn't see me

up on the ridge, waiting for the dawn
to melt my skin, blend me in
with stone and sand.

And when their boots marched over me,
they didn't hear the joke in the
crunching underfoot,

they didn't see me clinging to their laces
longing to be one of the lads.

"AS A GENERAL RULE WE DO NOT WILLINGLY EXPOSE CIVILIANS TO PHYSICAL DAMAGE"

Israeli border police spokesman 23rd April 2004

A boy of thirteen
leather buckled to the windscreen mesh
of a border policeman's armoured jeep,
protecting guns from stones;
an offensive defence.

Your knees are locked
against the engine's fever.
Your back is pressed
against the metal grill.
And from the corner of your eye
a tear streaks a passage through
the settled dust of olive groves
towards your muted mouth.

You are a shield
strapped cold to the heat
of the warrior's advance.
Rigid on the frontline
exposed to damage.
Silent in the grip of the battle.

A PALESTINIAN BOY IS STOPPED
BY AN ISRAELI SOLDIER

The boy is a butterfly on a light box
trying to hide the colour of his wings.

The soldier thinks he sees the ghosts of stones,
points his gun at puddles shaped like countries.

The boy slithers clenched fingers
inside the long sleeves of a yellow shirt
crosses right foot over left foot
feels his smallest toes touching.

The soldier thinks he sees the ghosts of stones,
points his gun at puddles shaped like countries.

The boy wobbles on a broken water pipe,
leans a handless arm against the wall.
The plastic flowers on his sandals stare
like bloodshot eyes.

The soldier thinks he sees the ghosts of stones,
points his gun at puddles shaped like countries.

The boy is trying to hide the colour
of his wings. He wonders if his body
will fall back or forward, what stains
a puddle makes on a yellow shirt.

AFTER QANA – JULY 30th 2006

I saw the lunchtime news and now

my arms ache with the dead weight of children whose bodies,
one by one, out of the rubble, I have not carried.

My fingers clench against one shoulder and under the bent knees
of a dead girl whose body in pink pyjamas, I have not lifted –

her head thrown back, her eyes closed against the dust –
whose cold hand against my chest, I have not felt.

Despair lands like a bloated pigeon on the acacia tree,
drags down delicate branches, scatters the leaves;

hope disappears over my garden wall like a dragonfly,
as the leaves of the Virginia creeper turn red too soon

and underneath the trellis where the jasmine creeps,
the buddlea drips with purple tears and the butterflies don't care.

Fifty-four civilians, mostly children killed
in an Israeli air-strike on a village in South Lebanon

A WAY OF RELIGION

When belief was a bedrock and counting was a way of religion,
I reckoned my way down through ten commandments,
nine ways of being accessory to another's sin,
eight Beatitudes, seven sacraments, six precepts of the church,
five decades of the rosary, four cardinal virtues,
three in one god (a mystery), two states of sin,
until I reached the one true God – with him I bargained.

Each night, hands joined beneath a shroud of blankets,
I bartered prayers and promises in secret pacts with God:
Keep me safe from the gap in the curtains; the faces
at the window; the ghost on the back of the door
that hangs like a dressing gown until the lights are out;
and if I die before I wake, save me from the flames and
take my soul to heaven or better still, don't let me die.

Nowadays religion's gone, communication lines are down
there's only counting left and no more bargaining with God,
but I light ten-pence candles, feel the sigh of wax pressed
into metal, then settle in the hush of a Cathedral's polished pew.
Two rubber soles squeak in motion, halt to genuflect, then
squeak again. The low-heeled ladies of the church clip clip
towards the altar. I count angels carved in stone
and lower the kneeler. It creaks for want of oil.

THE POWER OF FIVE

Counting five, inheriting power from the base of ten,
subjugating the base of four. Like the missionaries
teaching sins that never existed, in numbers that never existed,
bringing their rules and confessionals and stories of five loaves.
The two fish in the story were just a concession to the past

of a people who counted fish two by two in bundles of four.
The priests halved them into the catch of one hand
rather than two, to perpetrate the myth of the right hand
not knowing what the left hand does, to overturn

the balance of their ancient rituals that joined twos together
in bonds of co-operation and the oldest stratum of counting.
So that they lost even the words to say their own numbers
while the power of fives and tens took over
decimalising the world in subjugation.

Counting five in my hand I see it colonise my thumb
into digit identity, call it a finger, close it into a fist.
Like the Pentagon, always the rule of might.
still smothering the twos and fours in the power of five.

CINNAMON ROOTS

Cinnamon, sweet wood spice, once traded like gold,
when I look for my roots I find you, yellowish brown
like my winter skin, native of Sri Lanka, growing wild
in the jungles of the Kandy Highlands.

Fourteen ninety-two, Columbus never finds you,
sailing westwards to the lands of the Arawak Indians –
he promises spices and gold, trophies for a Spanish Queen.
Brings her Taino slaves as gifts.

But Portugal travels East to an island that falls like
a teardrop from the tip of India. Finds your soft sweetness,
wraps it in hard cash, grows rich on your rarity,
founding a spice trade, that deals in blood.

The Dutch make plantations to tame your wild fragrance
that can never sweeten their breath. Demand quotas of your bark,
enforced by death and torture. Burn down your August harvest,
fabled fuel of the phoenix fire, to keep up the prices.

Dutch East India becomes British East India.
Your acres grow in the rain and heat of Sri Lanka,
filling the coffers of the British Empire.

Nineteen ninety-two I buy your ground aroma in pre-packed jars,
fry you with aubergines and coriander, look for my roots,
find you yellowish brown, like my winter skin, native of Sri Lanka
growing wild in the jungles of the Kandy Highlands.

HOUSES OF LETTERS

Eyes, like dried-up lakes, want
rain, torrents, floods,
great gushing waves
to flow and fill the hollow
orange to indigo on the clouds' horizon.

I want to be there. I want to stay
in the sky forever, watching the sun
rise beyond the silver strip.
I want words to jump from envelopes
become arms around a dying friend.

Flying into the southern hemisphere,
close to the night; crescent moon
smiles at southern star, reflecting
on a tip of wing and Africa
beneath the haze.

I watch her sleep, shudder shallow breaths,
catch rays of sun, in copper hair,
touch her face, prepare myself to let her go
along with dreams of two women
growing old, in houses full of letters.

HOSPITAL STREET

Hospital Street has a roof
that sings piped music to the shifting
mass of wheelchairs, pyjama'd patients,
nurses, doctors, porters, cleaners
and visitors like us.

We fall in with the collective
measured speed, in this vision
of a moving walkway, where each
step calmly traces the distance
between breast clinic, cancer clinic.

We walk slowly, two women with
a common friend. We have left her sleeping,
taken the swift steel lift to Hospital Street.
We have left her on floor nine, 495, the cancer ward,
but no-one ever says the name.

Hospital Street is floor five. An artery through
Johannesburg General, an endless corridor
of human traffic. We walk steadily, two women,
with a common friend, who sleeps in 495,
absorbing multicolours through her veins.

We do not know each other well, but we
talk as if we do, our heads close together,
comfort our mutual pain, retelling cancer tales.
Hospital Street moves slowly by measuring
the distance between life and death.

LANDSLIDE

Came too soon, like a landslide.
Fingertips white, clinging onto boulders,
seeping tears dried under falling dust.

Silence waits. Night voices drone
in endless chasms of shadowy blue.
Anger lurks red, wants to be held,

slips, shapeless, through my fingers.
Her death has left me floundering,
thirst swells my tongue. I want to swallow.

THE MORTUARY

Ten days they kept her cold in the mortuary waiting
for officialdom to verify her death and I dreamed her
every night to save her from the loneliness.

I searched through rooms of corpses reeking of
formaldehyde until I found her. Her coffin was open
and her face was covered with Cape daisy petals.

Each time I found her, I dreamed her back alive
so I could tell her socialist-materialist body
that spirits did exist.

THE FUNERAL

It was her legal next-of-kin who gave the nod.
There were no songs, no speeches, only
quiet breathing and the whisper of the coffin
creeping through brass doors to burn.

The three of us, curled close on the callous
wooden pew, tried to snatch a glimpse
of who we were in her short life; two friends
who shared her secrets and the sad-eyed boy
who loved her like a son.

Then it was over. Too silent, too ordered
for the riot of our grief that stomped outside
to search among the gravestones for a place
to lay the chaos of our feelings. All we found
were neat slabs scattered in the tidy green,
controlled and clipped around the edges.

THE COLOUR OF HER EYES

Can't remember the colour of her eyes,
found her in yellow, trying to shine,
but the light in her eyes had wilted.

Saw grey cancer's rigid corset suck
the sparkle from her eyes, scrape
the song from her voice, break her wings.

Pushed her into the sunshine, wrapped
in thick dark clothes, to cover her regrets,
nothing to cover mine, raw in the yellow heat.

Watched her float away, a slow bubble,
out of reach, translucent skin reflecting rainbows,
couldn't catch the sparkle of her eyes.

LAST VISIT TO THE HOSPICE

I held his hand, it was the only thing to do,
as I swallowed all the words I'd planned,
and quenched his quiet thirst with sips of water.

After years of push and pull between us,
his wishes I could never have fulfilled,
I held his hand; it was the only thing to do.

No more disappointments, no more questions,
I travelled with him on the open road to death
and quenched his quiet thirst with sips of water.

The ward TV screen flickered daytime soaps;
I closed my eyes and felt the swoop of swallows;
I held his hand; it was the only thing to do.

He was on the edge of heaven, talking to the dead
I, the non-believer, stayed there with him
and quenched his quiet thirst with sips of water.

In the end it seems that all I'd ever wanted
was to hold his hand in comfort, so
I held his hand; it was the only thing to do,
and quenched his quiet thirst with sips of water.

ONE OF THE OLD SONGS

Sing me one of the old songs, Mum,
a song that smells of soapsuds, Ella,
Sarah, Nat King Cole over the two-beat
rhythm of a swaying motor, wrapping
your voice, like arms around me.
Sing me one of the old songs, Mum.

Tell me a tale of the old days, Mum,
a tale that lights your eyes, dances your voice
through musicals and country lanes on horseback,
when you shone your beauty in my father's eyes,
joining two continents in marriage.
Tell me a tale of the old days, Mum.

Give me one of your old looks, Mum,
one of those knowing looks, from the
corner of your eye, those *I'm saying nowt*,
Don't be so daft looks that speak volumes,
without a word.
Give me one of your old looks, Mum.

Hold me with your soft hands against
your beating heart, that cried for nine years
after my father's death, until the tears
filled your lungs, took your breath away.
Give me a song, give me a tale, give me a look,
hold me again, before I say goodbye.

FURTHER DETAILS OF LOSS

(Reasonably priced family home. Parents deceased. No chain)

1940's semi-detached home, located
at the quiet end of the road,
over the hill from the noisy end.
A front porch of glass and brick construction
for a mother who hated draughts,
part double-glazed by a DIY father, who economised.

His home-made cupboards have made way
for modern wall and base units in a kitchen
that was always too small for a mother
who squeezed herself between washing machine and oven
to sift and blend, baste and mash, chop and fry
three meals a day; apple pie and cake at weekends.

The lounge, always known as the front room, is measured
into original leaded stained glass half-bay window,
once a picture book for sick children in bed downstairs.
The original wood-surround fireplace listens alone now;
comforts itself with memories of the duster's caress
in this aching room, filled with the sighs of a widow.

The dining room clings on to happier memories
of Christmas and anniversary family meals,
kept safe in a corner of the built-in cupboard,
once crammed with dusters, tins and games
that tumbled out of its carefully opened door.
A full-frame window searches the garden

for a child, smiling, ankles crossed, on a rusty swing.

TIGHTROPES FOR THE DANCING SPARROWS

Sleep-slowed hands grope for light in another grey day
as early morning slices through my dreams. Outside,
a sycamore with falling leaves is framed by telephone wires
that are tightropes for the dancing sparrows.

Beyond this moment of selfless reflection
there is a sleeping child to coax from warm pyjamas,
a reluctant schoolgirl to steer through slow spoonfuls
of honeyed porridge.

I wonder when we leave, before I join the clutch of mothers
who clatter up our street with urgent, late-for-school voices,
will I remember to stop, bend down, take her arm and point
her fingers and her eyes skywards to the dancing sparrows?

ABOUT THE AUTHOR

Seni Seneviratne is a writer, singer, photographer and performer. She was born in Leeds, Yorkshire in 1951 to an English mother and Sri Lankan father. She has been writing poetry since her early teens and was first published in 1989.

Her poetry and prose is published in the UK, Denmark, Canada and South Africa. Her work has been published in *Flora Poetica* (Chatto & Windus); *The Redbeck Anthology of British South Asian Poetry* (Redbeck); *Healing Strategies for Women at War* (Crocus); *Language of Water, Language of Fire,* (Oscars); *Talking Black,* (Cassell); *Bad Reputation*, (Yorkshire Arts Circus); *Miscegenation Blues* (Sister Vision Press) and children's anthologies – *Masala: Poems from India, Bangladesh, Pakistan & Sri Lanka* (Macmillan); *Free My Mind*, (Hamish Hamilton).

She won second prize in the Margot Jane Memorial Poetry Prize, Onlywomen Press. She has given readings and performances in Vancouver, Cape Town, and around England. Her poetry has been broadcast on radio and recorded on audiotape, 'Climbing Mountains' and CD, 'Seven Sisters'. Her photography has appeared in *Feminist Arts News*, *Autograph Open Photography Show*, *Signals Changing Exhibition* and in a solo exhibition, *Moving Words*

Her collaborations include a mixed media installation , 'Memoried Mosaics' which was exhibited in Sheffield's Open Up event in 2004 and at Outwood Grange College, Wakefield; an art song for piano and voice, 'Dandelion Clocks' was commissioned for Leeds Leider Festival and performed in October 2005; 'A Wider View', verse accompanied by saxophone quartet, was commissioned for Leeds launch of Architecture Week, June 2006.

OTHER RELATED POETRY TITLES

Raman Mundair
A Choreographer's Cartography
ISBN: 1-84523-051-5; pp. 128; pub. March 2007; Price: £8.99

Raman Mundair's second collection of poems sees her expanding her territory to create a new poetic geography. Her voice dances from her love for the language and life of the Shetland Islands through the anguish of war to the movement of people and the crossing of boundaries. She brings to all a combination of passion and compassion, sensitivity and sensuality.

The collection encompasses poems written in the Shetland dialect, narratives of thwarted desire and a sequence of poems which explore the dynamics and historical by-ways of the waltz.

"Mundair conveys a vivid and memorable sense of self, and a truly poetic intimation of a dimension beyond the sharply focused moment. This voice deserves to be widely heard."

– Michael Mitchell, University of Warwick

Also by Raman Mundair
Lovers, Liars, Conjurers and Thieves
ISBN: 1-900715-80-5; pp. 96; pub. 2003; Price: £7.99

From beginnings secreted in the folds of her mother's sari, transplanted to England to struggle with the rough musicality of Mancunian vowels, Raman Mundair, a Punjabi Alice, found no true reflection of herself, no wonderland, but mirrors which dissolved, shrank and obscured her size. In these poems she creates her own universe and dissects its realities in all their complex, tragic and surreal forms.

At the heart of the collection is an acute sensitivity to the body: hurt, aroused, desired, ignored. Her poems spill out from this centre: to the physical memory of domestic violence, the intense joys of intimacy and love, and the pain of their rejection, to a passionate concern with the body politic. Here the approach is oblique, metaphorical, observant of the details that carry the poems beyond political statement.

"*She is constantly sensual... tempered by a delicate care for detail, a quality of consideration that engages in the philosophical in sometimes complex ways...*"

– Kwame Dawes

Jeanne Ellin
Who Asks the Caterpillar?
ISBN:1-900715-96-1,pp.104; pub. 2004; price: £8.99

Jeanne Ellin writes consciously as an Anglo-Indian, part of an 'invisible' group that has generally sunk its identity in a general Britishness. She, by contrast, has used her work to explore her sense of Indian origins, but finds her real source of inspiration in the ideas of anomaly and placelessness, themes she explores both directly and obliquely in her poetry. She writes of being 'cell deep... an elephant's child', but also that 'home is a land/ whose texture my feet have forgotten'. But this sense of placelessness also offers the strangers' right 'to a place at every table' and the challenge of living without 'family hand-me-downs', when each day must begin with a naked newness. More obliquely, she uses the mythical figure of the merchild/merechild to explore this sense of inbetweeness; and focuses, in the title poem, on the pleasures and pains of transformation, where after 'a lifetime of voracious consuming' the caterpillar suddenly finds itself as 'an ethereal being' and complains 'I didn't sign up for this spiritual stuff'.